INTRODUCTION

G000022924

Chipmunks are ground or terrestrial animals, but they also forage in trees. In this sense they can be considered to be intermediate between the tree squirrels, for example the Grey and Red Squirrels, and true ground-dwelling squirrels such as the prairie dog.

All chipmunks have large internal cheek pouches rather like the hamster, black and white facial stripes and a varying number of stripes on the back and sides of the body.

Chipmunks are found in North America with the single exception of one species that is widespread in Eurasia and has been introduced to some areas of Europe. It is this species that is commonly known as the Siberian Chipmunk.

At one time chipmunks were placed into two genera: *Eutamias* for the chipmunks of Western North America and Eurasia, and *Tamias* for those of Eastern North America. Most authorities still retain both these genera. However, recent evidence indicates that all chipmunks are so closely related that this separation is unwarranted. I don't really think that this matters to us, as pet owners, but it may explain why you may find that some books give different names to the same animals.

A tame chipmunk will come to greet you when you approach its cage. A wild chipmunk usually will keep away from you.

The name chipmunk is of uncertain origin. Usually it is attributed to the chip call note of the members of the genus; more plausibly, it was derived from an American Native Indian word 'achitaman' or 'chetaman' which, I am told, means 'head first,' in reference to the way that the chipmunk descends tree trunks.

To my mind, chipmunks make lively, wonderful companions whether you are keeping them in the home or in an outdoor complex. One word of warning: once you own a chipmunk you may feel that there is no other pet for you and you will soon be adding others or not wishing to part with any babies that yours produce. It is a sad situation having to part with the babies, but there does come a point when some have to go.

As I mentioned before, the major part of this book is about the Siberian Chipmunk, *Eutamias sibiricus*, mainly because this is the most easily obtained species and the species that has been retained in captivity for the longest period of time. However, nearly all the species and subspecies mentioned can be treated in the same way.

Chipmunks love treats, and by hand-feeding the treats you develop a bond with the animal.

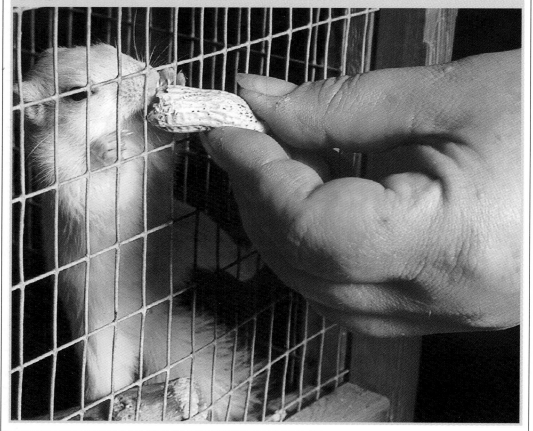

HOUSING

This chapter is about the type of accommodation that is required, not only by the Siberian Chipmunk, but also by the other species that I shall be talking about later in this book. Naturally, some species and even individuals have different housing requirements than others, and I shall deal with these under the appropriate headings.

In the wild chipmunks prefer to live in underground tunnels and burrows with a nesting chamber in or under hollow tree stumps.

A suitable outdoor home for chipmunks should be large, high, wooden with wire caging. Photo by Michal Gilroy.

They line their nests with soft foliage for warmth and comfort. Generally, each pair has its own nesting area. It does appear, at least in some species, that chipmunks live in fairly close association with other pairs or families.

Bearing this in mind, in captivity chipmunks are best housed outside in large, high, wooden and wire cages rather along the lines of bird aviaries. However, this is not the only way in which they may be kept and many people keep them in very much smaller cages than this. Certainly I would not like to say to someone living in an apartment or flat that they can't have a chipmunk because they don't have a garden. Chipmunks do very well indeed in this type of situation; it is only that the outdoor aviaries can be so much bigger than those indoors. For this reason I shall try to give you as many ideas on how to house your animals as I have used or have been suggested to me. Any measurements you see in the text are regarded as the minimum size that I would give to my own animals. However, the one rule that I would suggest is that the bigger the cage that you can provide, the better.

ALL WIRE INDOOR CAGE

This type of cage is limited only by the size that you can either buy or make and, more important, the amount of space that you have available. I would suggest that the *minimum* size is 60cm high by 20cm square (24 x 8in). Very few commercial cages are made for chipmunks, but they are available, often adapted from cages originally designed for chinchillas. However, these are ideal after branches, nest boxes, and so on have been added. One thing to double check is the width between the bars of the cage: make sure that they are no further apart than 1cm (0.4in).

Of course, you may like to make a cage of your own. I have found that the easiest way to do this is to make it out of an aviary wire called Monoweld or Twiweld or Weldmesh. This is a strong, squared mesh that is able to support itself, thus not needing any wooden or metal framing. It is fastened together using special pliers and clips known as C clips. I would recommend a cage as tall as it is wide but this does, of course, depend on the area in which the cage is to be sited. Cut a hole in one side of the cage and place a piece of mesh at least 10cm (4in) larger than the hole over it as a door. This can be fastened to the cage along one edge using the clips to create a hinge. A fastening can be created easily using the sort of wire frame

If you use nest boxes, they should be securely fastened to the wire.

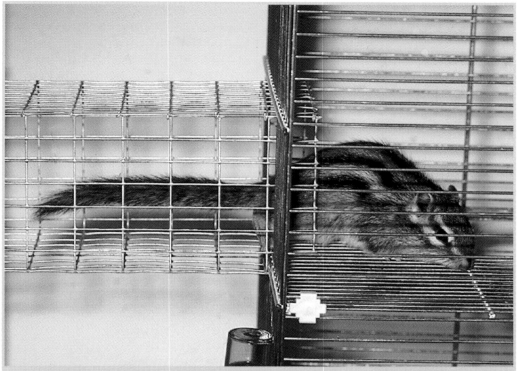

A wire run can connect two cages. This is especially useful for breeding. Photo by Michael Gilroy.

(sold in most department stores) for hanging small plates on the wall. A series of simple shelves may be placed inside the cage at various heights either by using wood (which will be chewed eventually), or by stretching more mesh between three of the walls. Twigs and branches can be provided for climbing, as can thick rope. The cage should have an all-wire bottom and this can be elevated a few centimetres on wood to enable droppings and urine to fall onto newspaper or sawdust on a tray below.

A nest box should be provided for each animal and these should be hung inside the cage, or outside with a suitable hole cut in the wire to allow access to the animals. Nest boxes can either be made or purchased. It is unlikely that you will find a nest box that is sold specifically for chipmunks, so look for those sold for budgies, lovebirds or small parrots.

OUTDOOR SHEDS OR AVIARIES

There are several different ways of arranging the outdoor accommodation for chipmunks; a large outdoor area attached to a shed with a small indoor area or vice versa, or an area total outdoors but in a sheltered spot with no attached shed but very well-built frostproof nest boxes. These can be purpose-built or adapted from bird aviaries. They can all be of different sizes to suit your own situation.

The aviaries themselves may be very simple or very complex, depending on the ability of the builder or what you can afford to buy. I would suggest that you try to have one that is pleasing to look at both to yourself and to others. Nothing is worse than the enclosure in which you keep your much-loved pets being so ugly that people don't remember the animals after their visit, only 'that awful shed.'

My own favourite is a rectangular outdoor area with a small shed attached. The outside area should have a paved or well-wired floor to prevent the chipmunks burrowing out or wild rodents and other creatures burrowing in. Then, around the entire area, I like to see a double row of bricks on which the wire framework stands. Ideally, the height should be for you rather than the chipmunks; after all, you will be entering the shed and run to see and be with the animals. There is nothing more uncomfortable than standing for a period with your back bent. Therefore if you are 6' I would suggest that the height of the roof be 6'4".

Any access door should be covered by an entrance porch; however, should your garden be small this may be resolved by having the entrance to the run via the shed.

Chipmunks seem to like pine cones. This is a healthy, alert animal.

A White investigates the top of its new nest box.

I would suggest that the shed be at least 1.8 x 1.2m (6 x 4ft) with an outdoor enclosure of at least 1.2m (4ft) square but, ideally, 3.6m x 3.6m (12 x 6ft) or 3.6 x 1.2m (12 x 4ft). The shed should be mounted on a paved area or similar floor. The shed roof should slope away from the enclosure and should be of wood with felt or weatherproof covering; never use a shed with a metal roof as this is both too hot and too noisy for chipmunks.

Approximately one-third to one-half of the outside area roof and all the north-facing wall should be covered by stout plastic on the outside to protect the inhabitants (and you, when you are feeding them), from the worst of the weather. There should be two entrances from the shed to the outside area, one at ground level and one at about your own shoulder height. The latter should be within easy reach of a branch within the outside area.

The outside area itself should have a floor well covered with peat litter or peat and/or bark chippings in which the chipmunks can dig and bury their food. It should be furnished with a good amount – as much as you can get in – of branches, twigs, hollow logs and so on. These should be washed before being included in the run and should be of a type of wood such as apple or

Hay makes a comfortable bedding, and chipmunks seem to enjoy the hay because it is so similar to the bedding they would make themselves.

pear. You can leave on the leaves as they will add interest for the animals. One nest box per individual should be placed along one wall of the outside aviary. I suggest that they be at about your own shoulder height, so that you can inspect them easily. Also they should be all at the same height as this prevents the chipmunks fighting over possession of the highest one. I recommend that they are at least two chipmunks' body lengths apart, for the same reason.

The interior of the shed should be divided into two, or possibly three, different areas. The part nearest the outside run should be wired off to allow a floor to roof indoor cage. This will give the chipmunks an area in which to exercise during bad weather, with nest boxes available to each animal and allowing free movement and access from both the inside and outside areas. The rear and major part of the shed can be used as either a storage area for food and food preparation or divided yet again to give a small, all-indoor run that can be used for individuals that for some reason have to be separated from the main population. The shed should have an outside window and this should be wired over, yet still able to be opened to allow

This is an excellent nest box for chipmunks.

Nest boxes for chipmunks must be insulated and lined with bedding to keep the chipmunk warm and secure.

ventilation. The door of the shed should also be screened so that it can be left open in good weather.

Nesting materials should be provided for whatever cage or enclosure is decided upon. I suggest that this is soft, sweet meadow hay. As already mentioned, peat is the best floor covering, but this is getting more difficult to obtain and any of the substitutes on the market are just as good. Hay absorbs urine and faeces better than wood shavings,

although for an indoor cage that needs to be cleaned more often, wood shavings are just as good. Food should be provided in a strong, heavy earthenware bowl that cannot be tipped over easily, although some food can be scattered on the floor, particularly of the aviaries, to give the animals something to do in hunting for it. Water should be available at all times, provided in water bottles attached to the outside of the cage or aviary. This allows quick and easy replacement and also prevents the bottles from being chewed.

Cages, both indoor and out, should be scrubbed at least twice, if not four times, a year with some form of disinfectant, then rinsed with clean water as many times as it takes to absorb the smell of the solution. Nest boxes should be cleaned out periodically; this is particularly easy to do just after a litter has been weaned. Generally, chipmunks have very little odour and require little in the way of cleaning.

ESCAPES

Should one of your chipmunks escape in the house, there's little problem in returning it to its cage; however, should this happen from an outdoor enclosure, then you may have trouble. If only one escapes, you may find that, if left alone and given access to the aviary or cage, then it will return to its own nest box before nightfall. However, should a pair escape, then they are unlikely to return. If they breed and thus establish a colony, you would be liable to prosecution. Chipmunks are able to survive in the United Kingdom and they have already established themselves in various European countries from escaped pets.

Branches strategically located near the nest box will assist older chipmunks, as well as the young, in leaving the nest box, to get in and out.

DIET AND FEEDING

When and how often to feed chipmunks leads to as many different views as there are owners of the animals. Ideally, chipmunks should be fed at least once a day and twice if there is a large group, but this does depend on your life style. Animals kept in outdoor enclosures are much more likely to go to bed at dusk than those kept inside the house, and are therefore less likely to be inclined to feed at night. In normal circumstances, chipmunks are diurnal, that is, they are awake mainly during the day and sleep at night or during bad weather.

I usually feed my animals in the evening both in summer and winter as for me this is the most convenient time. My animals are now used to this regime and expect their food at this time.

As with the majority of rodents, the chipmunk's basic diet is made up of various seeds and cereals, with the addition of fruits and vegetables and, to a lesser extent, some form of protein. The latter is

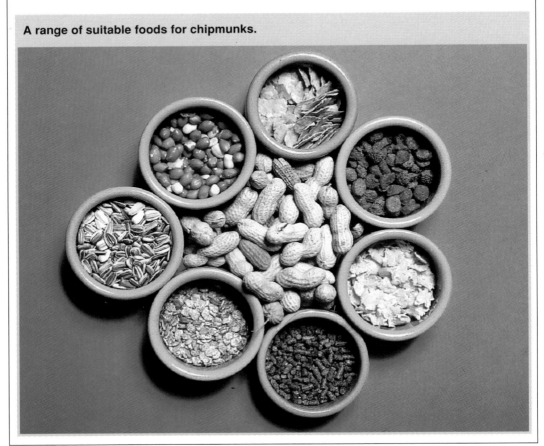

A range of suitable foods for chipmunks.

If there is such as thing as a favorite food for chipmunks, it would be peanuts in many cases.

the cause of some debate, which I shall deal with later. Firstly, let us deal with the basics: seeds and cereals.

It is no longer a problem to obtain a special mix for a number of different rodents including chipmunks, and this is often sold as chipmunk and squirrel mix. Although this is a good basic diet, it does tend to be very heavily stocked with sunflower seeds and peanuts. Although the chipmunks like it, it is not a balanced diet and tends to make the animals very fat.

SO WHAT IS A BALANCED DIET?

In the wild, the chipmunks' diet would vary greatly depending on their habitat, but would include seeds, nuts, vegetation, the bark and shoots of trees, berries, insects, and occasionally small birds, eggs and even mice – a very varied diet.

In captivity, we must reflect this by what we place in the cage, as by keeping the animals confined they are unable to forage for any additions that they may require. After all, they are unable to tell us exactly what they need.

Carbohydrates

These are a quickly digested, readily absorbed source of energy and are very important in the diet of small animals of any type that tend to spend much of their time jumping and bouncing about. Approximately 50% of their intake should be made up of a mixture of cereals such as oats, wheat, barley and corn. Carbohydrates are also contained in dog biscuits and some seeds such as millet.

Excessive intake of carbohydrates, beyond the animals' daily needs, will be turned into fats for storage. While the chipmunks need a comfortable layer of fat to protect them from the cold, they should not be allowed to gain too much weight. On the other hand, too little carbohydrate intake will cause the animal to obtain its energy needs by breaking down the fat reserves.

Fats

Fats are needed in the diet to provide essential fatty acids and to act as a vector for certain fat-soluble vitamins, for example A, D, E and K. As mentioned above, too much fat is bad as it tends to be laid down around the internal organs and under the skin, adding weight to the body, inhibiting mobility and thus adding strain to the limbs. Insufficient fats in the diet, however, will result in reproductive infertility, poor skin and dull coats. The major source of fats in the diet is fat-rich nuts and seeds, for example, peanuts, almonds, hazel, acorns, beech masts, walnuts and pine seeds.

You can overdo feeding by offering too much food. It is not good practice to allow the food to accumulate, rot and attract insects.

Chipmunks characteristically sit up to feed, as this White chipmunk demonstrates.

With walnuts and other hard-shelled seeds you may find it necessary to break open the shells for the animals before you feed them, although attempting to open some will help to keep their teeth in good shape. Sunflower seeds are high in oils and are a firm favourite, but they should not be fed in great amounts because of their very fattening properties and very low levels of calcium. Corn is also a very good source of fats and may be fed in a variety of different ways, both dried and fresh. Eggs are another good source and a single egg yolk between two animals once a week is ideal.

Don't let your animals bully you into feeding what they like the most. You will find that sunflowers and peanuts will be eaten first and other items left. When hungry the chipmunks will eat these but, rather like naughty children, they will try to persuade you that they hate them and would much rather have some more sweets.

Protein
In the body muscles are built up and repaired by the proteins taken from the diet. In active animals, the muscles are in a constant state of wear and tear. Proteins are required to form

enzymes, hormones which ensure that vital functions within the body are carried out and to renew the blood and cells.

Wild rodents obtain proteins from both animal and plant sources in their varied diets. In order to provide these in the diet a number of different foods may be given. As already mentioned, eggs are ideal, and the white is a very good source of protein, as are various types of insects, for example, mealworms and grasshoppers. In an outdoor aviary you will undoubtedly see your chipmunks catching and eating flies and moths. Proteins are also found in various vegetable matter such as nuts, peas and lentils, fruit and vegetables. You will also find that you are able to buy protein pellets suitable for feeding to small rodents in your pet shop and included in pre-mixed rodent foods. However, I find that these are not much liked by the chipmunks.

Vitamins and Minerals

These are found in a wide range of foods, particularly fresh fruit and vegetables: oranges, apples, pears, grapes, various soft fruits, bananas, bean sprouts, carrots, sweet potatoes, tomatoes, and a lot more. Don't forget the various

The containers in which you offer your pet chipmunk its food should be heavy and easy to clean.

Tame chipmunks return to their cages for feeding.

hedgerow fruits in the autumn, such as rose hips and hawthorn berries, and some garden flowers are also liked. I have one chipmunk that loves marigolds and another that likes nasturtiums. One word of warning: If you feed any fruits containing stones such as plums or peaches, ensure that you remove the stone first as it contains a toxin that chipmunks are unable to deal with.

Calcium

Although calcium should be provided in the diet naturally, you can provide additional supplements of both calcium and other minerals in the form of various powders and drops. Another very simple solution is to put a cuttlefish bone in the cage

Chipmunks like grapes, as well as most juicy fruits which are not citrus.

If you have a new chipmunk you can test its feeding likes and dislikes by offering it everthing you think it might enjoy and that you have available. Check out what he eats first...and most.

If you offer your pet chipmunk a treat every time you visit, the animal will eagerly look forward to your visits.

upon which the chipmunks can gnaw.

SUMMING UP

The above is a general idea of what should be in the diet of the animals in your care. Many other items may be added from time to time, and these can vary greatly. Basically, if you can eat it then it should be okay for the chipmunks, but if in doubt, leave it out!

HOW MUCH TO FEED?

Each chipmunk only eats about 30g (1oz) of food a day. Anything over and above this will be stored, so it is wasteful to offer too much to the animals, although too little is just as bad. They must have some extra food to store away and this gives them a sense of security. This is especially important in the autumn as hibernation approaches. At this point fighting may break out in large groups if food is in short supply.

Naturally, lactating and pregnant females require more food than a male or non-breeding female. If you are unsure whether or not there is a litter in the nest then add a small amount to the food supply just in case. Once you have had your animals for a while you will learn the amount that they will eat per day and be able to feed accordingly.

When it comes to feeding your pet, generally if it's okay for you it should be okay for your chipmunk.

THE SIBERIAN CHIPMUNK

There are a number of sub-species of the Siberian Chipmunk originating from various parts of the Far East. The species as a whole is described as ranging from the Berin Sea to the central Asian deserts, including Manchuria, Korea, Shatung and central China and the islands of Sakhalin, Iturup, and Hakkaido.

The official scientific description of the species as a whole reflects this very wide distribution and the fact that many different colour variations occur. The following is a combination of different descriptions and observations that I have made in the British Museum of Natural History. I hope that it will help you to understand the complexity of the question of where in the wild a particular animal may come from.

COLOUR

In the various species, the top of the head varies from greyish-buff chestnut to a more intense rust-brown with buff mottling. Eyes are surrounded by a white to whitish ring, and a whitish stripe with a buff tone at the margin runs from the ring to the nose. Another stripe runs from the top corner of the ring to the base of the ear. A chestnut-black-brown

Chipmunks are especially fond of grapes (below) and peanuts (facing page), so bring your chipmunk's favorite food every time you come to visit.

Peanuts and other nuts are favorite foods of the strong-toothed chipmunk.

stripe runs from the bottom margin of the ring to the ear. A dark-chestnut stripe is bordered by more chestnut of varying intensity from the muzzle, beneath the eye ring around the eye. The lower parts of the cheeks are sometimes more yellow-rust coloured. Behind the ears is ash grey with a rust tinge. Five chestnut-black longitudinal stripes run from the neck down the back. The middle stripe goes from the nape to the shoulder and continues to the middle of the back. The lateral stripes begin behind the base of the forelegs and continue to the sides of the buttocks. Between the five dark stripes there are four lighter stripes, the top part of the stripes being whitish buff and the lower part more reddish/rust-coloured. The intensity of the rust shade varies in the different sub-species, between cinnamon buff and cinnamon, sayal brown and orange cinnamon. The whole of the lower part of the back and the haunches are reddish rust varying in intensity. Yellowish rust tones are also present on the flanks. This colour is sharply defined from the dirty-white tone of the belly. The tail is chestnut grey, with the tips of the hairs white. The roots of these hairs are usually pale buff rust followed by

Chipmunks are much happier in a natural setting, in an aviary, in which evergreen trees are always available for climbing. Photo by Michael Gilroy.

Chipmunks eat wild berries in nature. Sometimes they become ill from eating poison berries. Photo by Michael Gilroy.

a broad black band and then white tip. There are also many hairs that are completely black with white tips. The feet tend to be grey chestnut buff and the claws are greyish. Whiskers are grey or black.

So that's it. To sum up, I have found that the chipmunks of the west and the island populations appear to be more sandy or cinnamon and also finer-boned than those of the northeast and Korea. Naturally others may disagree with me.

SIBERIAN CHIPMUNK GENETICS

As mentioned above, the colours of the Siberian vary greatly, but they do have something in common: they are all basically a reddish/brownish/ greyish colour commonly known as Agouti. It appears that these colour variations cannot be bred because by mating two reddish animals together, there is no certainty that reddish babies will occur even in later generations. There is however one exception to this, and that appears to be an animal called the Cinnamon.

Over the past few years this colour has appeared quite often in various litters and I believe that it may be descended from stock imported into the United Kingdom in the late 1960s and early 1970s from the Japanese island of Hokkaido. These individuals were slightly finer-boned than those of the mainland, and were described as more noticeably reddish/ cinnamon. Unfortunately stock of

A typical female chipmunk. Photo by Michael Gilroy.

A plump, pregnant, healthy female at the dinner table. Photo by Michael Gilroy.

this island race was not retained in separate populations from those of the mainland. Most of the animals in Great Britain are descended from animals obtained from Korea. However in recent years individuals have been born that are finer-boned and much more reddish/cinnamon in coloration than the normal Siberian. I feel that these may well be a throwback to the Hokkaido stock. As this has caused more and more interest I have attempted to gather some of these animals, breed them and compare notes with others. From this it does appear that you can develop a true breeding colour for cinnamon animals but, in order to do this, you must have either two cinnamon animals or a cinnamon and a cinnamon carrier or two carriers. This means that the cinnamon colour is what is known as a recessive gene, that can be covered or masked by the normal Agouti.

WHITE/DILUTE CHIPMUNKS

One true mutation does occur and this is indeed a recessive mutation. It is known as the White or Dilute. It is not an albino; it is a pale cream to white animal with pale beige stripes and tail and dark, almost black, eyes. A true albino would have no stripes and bright pink eyes.

The White animals prove to be a little less hardy than the normals, and can suffer in open aviaries from sunburn in very hot weather. But they are delightful animals, often much tamer and calmer than the normals. They can be smaller but this is usually due to inbreeding and this can be rectified by outcrossing a white animal to a normal. This will produce all-normal animals, some of which will be carrying white. If you mate these together or back to the whites you will again have white babies.

Recently I have been told of a number of different mutations in the Siberian Chipmunks, including Black, Blue, Lilac and Patched, but as yet I have not seen any of these animals nor have the people who have reported these colours shown any evidence to support their claims. I would dearly love to know more about any of these. So if you've seen them, please let me know.

SIBERIAN BEHAVIOUR

To understand the behaviour of our pets, I think that it is important to look at the behaviour of the wild species. In this way we can see more easily why certain things are required in their care. Much of the behaviour of the Siberians also applies to other species in this book.

In the wild, the Siberian is a diurnal animal. Its daily life appears to differ from season to

After discovering that your pet chipmunk prefers apples, you can use the apple to get his attention...

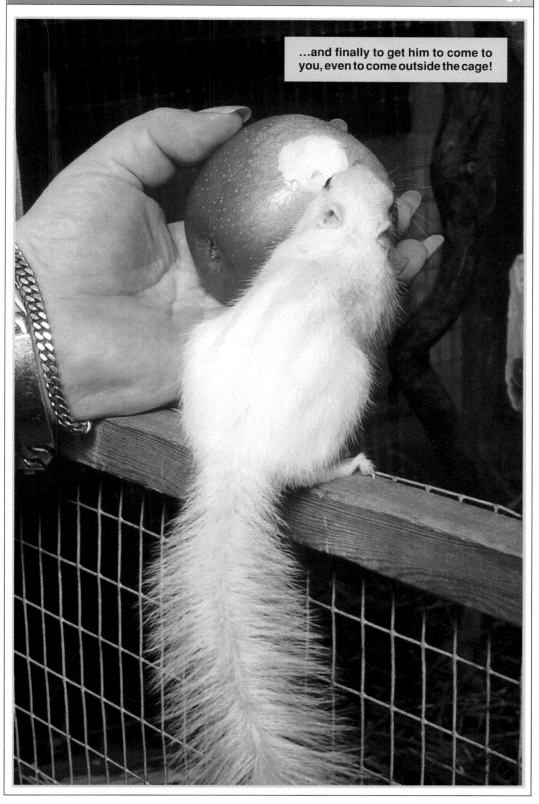

...and finally to get him to come to you, even to come outside the cage!

season and according to the weather of the day. In the spring, it comes out of its burrow only when the sun has had a chance to warm up the ground a little. The main period of activity is from approximately 10am to 4pm. By sunset they are usually back in their burrows. They also remain in them when the weather is wet or very windy. In summer, they are up and about just before daybreak, often as soon as it is light enough to see. They are very active – jumping, washing and chasing about in addition to the normal feeding and mating behaviour. Between noon and 2pm they appear to return to the burrows for a midday sleep, reappearing to remain active and feeding until sunset when they return to their burrows for the night.

In summer and autumn, they appear to be less concerned by the rain and wind than during the spring. This may be because the areas in which this species has been most commonly studied has quite a high rainfall level during these months, but that it is not particularly cold and thus not too unpleasant. During the autumn, it appears that the chipmunks' behaviour patterns are similar to those of the summer, making the most of the warm daylight hours to feed, collect and store food for the oncoming winter.

Winter behaviour really does appear to depend on where the animals are. In some areas of Siberia, they hibernate totally from October through to February, while in many other areas they are up and about, out of their burrows feeding whenever it is a mild day.

The burrows do not appear to be very complex. The entrance is usually at the base of a tree stump. The burrow descends at an angle of approximately 45°E immediately after the entrance. It then continues almost horizontally and ends in a rounded chamber, which contains the nest area. Side galleries appear to be rare and there are never more than three. The burrows usually only have one exit. The galleries are some 60–400cm (24–160in) long and the chamber about 20–40cm (8–15in) wide and 40–100cm (16–40in) below the ground. Some burrows have small corridors filled with excrement. Food reserves are kept in chambers, very rarely in the galleries. The nest is usually an open chamber with the bedding material in the centre. The entrance to the burrow is usually hidden by some form of vegetation.

HANDLING AND SEXING SIBERIANS

Unless obtained at a young age and well tamed, chipmunks do not like being handled in the true sense of the word and may even bite very hard. This is not to say that they cannot be tamed, even if obtained as adults. Far from it – many of them are very easy to handle, but winning the confidence of a chipmunk enough that it allows itself to be handled is much more difficult than taming a hamster, for example.

A head-on view of a healthy, pregnant chipmunk. Photo by Michael Gilroy.

There are no hard and fast rules – it requires care, patience and, above all, understanding, especially of the fact that some individuals will never allow themselves to be handled, however well they are treated. It is easier to tame an adult if you have large aviary type accommodation, one in which you can sit and allow the animals to come and smell, touch and climb on you, yet at the same time able to run away from you or keep their distance and thus feel safe. Merely by sitting and allowing the animals to come to you, you will find that gradually they begin to climb over you and take items of food from your hand. Eventually, some will start to push themselves up against your hand during this process, actually asking for you to stroke them. Never rush the process, never attempt to pick the animal up unless it is able to jump away from you and therefore not feel trapped. To be blunt, one silly mistake and taking things too quickly can undo a month's long hard work.

No one way of taming an animal is wrong or right. What may work with one may not with another. But one thing you must never do is to grab a chipmunk. This is what they hate above all else and they will bite and mean it.

A breeder with time and care will usually have gone to the trouble of hand taming his young stock. Not all have the time to tame all their stock, but animals bred from tame animals take far less time than those from untamed animals.

Hand-taming young homebred stock is a simple matter. Most females that are used to the presence of their owner will allow you to look into the nest box, even if they themselves are not hand-tamed. Once it is clear that the babies are moving around and about to open their eyes, at about 12 days or so, begin to gently lift them out of the nest box and get them used to your scent and feel of your hands on them. This does not have to be a very long session but ideally should take place every day. Once their eyes are open, continue this process and gradually you will find that they will be climbing all over you whenever you come within reach and will even allow you to do what their parents hate and clasp them around the body.

It is possible to pick some animals up by cupping or lifting by the scruff of the neck, but it is difficult and I would not advise it, especially with strange or newly acquired animals. Chipmunks are difficult to capture, even tame ones, especially in an outdoor enclosure. They are agile, to say the least, and a long chase without a break is extremely stressful and should be avoided at all costs. This is particularly true with pregnant or nursing females. The best way to capture them in this situation is with a soft butterfly net. This can be quickly and gently placed over the individual who is then gathered into the base of the net and brought to your chest. Be careful, as you are more likely to be bitten at this stage than at any other

A chipmunk baby, eight days old, but already starting to show stripes. Photo by Michael Gilroy.

time. I would advise that you obtain a pair of thick leather gloves for handling your untamed animals. Once you have netted your chipmunk place your hand firmly across its back and with the other hand supporting it underneath, left it from the net. It can also be lifted with the thumb and forefinger round the thick of the neck and the other hand supporting it.

To sex your chipmunk, gently turn it on to its back with the genitals facing outwards and one hand supporting it just below the forelimbs. Determine the sex by the distance between the anus and the genitals – the distance is greater in the male than the female. Of course an adult male will also be more easily distinguished by the presence of the testicles.

TWO THINGS TO REMEMBER:
    1. Never lift a chipmunk by its tail unless you hold it very close to the body or the chipmunk may shed and lose the tail.
    2. Chipmunks usually bite first and ask questions and say sorry later.

BREEDING

As already stated, chipmunks can be kept as breeding pairs or in groups of one male to two or three females or something along the lines of two males and six females. It is unwise to keep more males than females, as fighting will break out over the females when they come into season. Chipmunks are mature and ready for breeding in the spring of the year following their birth, that is, from six to twelve months of age depending on when they were born the previous year.

Breeding activity usually commences among animals in outside enclosures after the end of the winter, once the days begin to lengthen, usually from the beginning of March until September, with most of the matings occurring in April and May to produce the first litters and July and August for late ones.

Animals indoors may well begin a couple of months earlier as they usually do not bother with hibernation. In fact, they may even breed all year round, particularly if they have a constant source of artificial light. However, I would not advise you to allow your female to breed all year as this causes a great deal of stress and may lead to the shortening of her life span.

Once the females have decided that spring has arrived, they start to come into season. A female in heat makes no attempt to disguise the fact — far from it. She makes her condition quite plain by calling any available male with a high chirp. Once you have heard this you are unlikely to forget it. She will repeat this series of chirps at frequent intervals throughout the day and will mate with any male who can catch her. If you keep several animals in an outdoor enclosure, there may be outbreaks of fighting amongst the males as they vie for her favours. She may mate several males as they vie for her favours. She may mate several times at 5—10 minute intervals with one male and then lose interest in him and move to another. Thus if you wish to mate particular animals together you need to house them in pairs rather than groups.

Even if a mated male is losing interest in her, the female will usually flaunt herself in front of him. She struts stiff-legged around the branches with her tail fluffed out and lashing in a slightly annoyed manner until he regains his interest. At this point she dashes off across the cage calling over her shoulder for him to catch her. It is probably good for the males that she is only in this mood for a short time or their life span would be very short. The following day she will still be of interest to the males but will be aloof and certainly not allow them to mate.

A male chipmunk climbing the wire.

Chipmunks mating.
Photo by Michael Gilroy.

The gestation period is 28—35 days, although this is only a guideline and some females may not conform to it. This may also be due to the fact that the first matings of a breeding season may not be successful. Usually this is because the males are not yet in prime breeding condition and their testes have not fully descended.

External signs of pregnancy are not evident initially, but within the first 10 days there will be a slight enlargement of the lower mammary glands. After about 20—25 days, the glands further up the body become more prominent and the female may begin to look noticeably wide at the girth. The female remains active throughout the pregnancy.

Throughout the period the female builds up her nest box ready for the big day. At this time you must ensure that she is provided with lots of safe, warm nesting materials with which she can line her nest and a little extra food to hoard. She will need this store in her nest for the period immediately after she has given birth as she does not usually leave the young for the first 24 hours of their life. No matter how tame and trusting the female is with you, at this point do not disturb her. If you do she may

Chipmunks attempting to mate. Virgin animals often have trouble during their first mating experiences.

Locate your nest box near a tree branch so the chipmunk can jump onto the branch or use the branch to get to the nest box.

well abandon the young or even kill and eat them. Once she has given birth and is happy that the young are warm and comfortable and she is hungry or thirsty she will emerge from the box. At first she will not stay away from her babies for too long as they are unable to regulate their temperature and need mum to be their hot water bottle. Some females encourage the male to take turns in looking after the nest, particularly in a single pair situation.

Do not take a look; even when she has left the nest for the first time, she will still be very nervous for her young. Once she has been in and out of the nest a few times and returns to her normal feeding patterns in other areas of the cage you can take a quick peep through the side or roof of the nest box. It must be quick, for although the mother has ventured away she keeps her eye on the nest and will quickly return to see what you are up to. The young are usually buried under the layers of bedding material in order keep them warm. Be very careful and open the bedding slowly, taking great care not to touch the youngsters at this stage. As soon as they are uncovered they will begin to squeak in protest and move about in an attempt to get back under cover. If the female hears this she will return to the box. The first thing she will do is check the entrance hole to see if it has been disturbed as usually a female closes the hole as she leaves by pulling some of the bedding over the gap. Of course, you will not have disturbed this as you will be looking at the nest via either the removable roof or side of the nest box. Providing that you can leave the nest box almost as you found it, usually the female will not be too concerned and then you can look in on the babies every day.

One of my females usually sits on my shoulder while I remove the top of the box, almost demanding to know what I think of her babies today. Once I have finished my quick inspection, she takes the titbits of food I have brought for her and sits on top of the nest box to eat them. She never checks the babies until the food is finished.

By the time that the babies are one week old, they are gaining a fine downy coat which will be fully through by about 14—16 days. Their eyes, however, are still closed and they blunder about the nest in great agitation when tampered with. The little squeaks with which they greeted you at a few days old have stopped by this time and usually they are very silent in the nest. Their eyes open at about 26—28 days, which is quite late in their development. Do not worry if one eye opens one day and the other the next as this is quite normal.

From about five weeks of age, occasionally earlier, the youngsters start to venture out of the box. At this time it is important to ensure that there is plenty of climbing material about, or at least a platform near to the nest box entrance for them to rest on. During this first week they learn to forage for their own food and find the water supply.

The mother shows the young the different types of food on offer and at the same time she is still suckling them on their return to the nest. However, by six weeks of age the mother's milk has dried up and the young are on their own as far as food is concerned.

I do not remove the babies from the parents until they are at least eight weeks of age, and then only if either they have a new owner waiting for them or the enclosure is too small to accommodate both the adults and the youngsters. If the cage or aviary is large then they can stay with their parents for a while, but do ensure that they are provided with enough space and a nest box each.

LONGEVITY

Chipmunks are relatively long-lived creatures compared with many other small rodents kept as pets. On the whole it would appear that females live longer than males. Most animals reach the age of four or five years, but some have been recorded as reaching the age of nine or even ten years.

REQUIREMENTS FOR SUCCESSFUL BREEDING

Not every pair of chipmunks produces young. There are various reasons for this. There are a number of different stages of reproduction and all these stages must be successful for a litter to be produced. Therefore if a pair appears to be getting on well yet fails to breed, check the following:

- climate and day length are important; do not expect animals in outdoor aviaries to breed too early
- cage size is important, especially with regard to litter size; animals in larger cages appear to produce larger litters than those in small indoor cages
- cage furnishings are important; extra nest boxes should be provided, at least one per individual and all at approximately the same height
- the presence of other rodents can prevent breeding
- with animals kept indoors, televisions cause stress because of their high frequency.

GROUPING

Pairs

By far the most successful grouping of the Siberian Chipmunk in captivity for breeding is the pairing of two animals of the opposite sex. This sounds a strange statement to make, but not everyone regards a pair as a male and a female. Many people, dealers included, regard a pair as two individuals, regardless of sex. However, even two animals of the opposite sex cannot be guaranteed to breed. As stated elsewhere, it doesn't really matter what type of cage is provided, as long as it meets the requirements of the individuals it contains. It is true to say that, on the whole, successful breeding is achieved more often in an outside cage than in an indoor one.

If both individuals are new to you, and are also new to each other, they are quite likely to fight when they are introduced; therefore it is better to introduce them to a new cage at the same time. The uncertainty of their new surroundings often prevents fighting. This is more true for individuals of breeding age than those under 12 months of age.

Should you purchase a breeding or established pair, introduction to a new cage usually presents no problems at all. If, however, you already possess one of a pair and then wish to introduce a new partner, I have found that the most successful way is to allow the male the run of the cage or aviary for at least 24 hours before the female is introduced. You can introduce the male into the

A male chipmunk investigating the female chipmunk. As with most living things, the male is the more aggressive of the pair. Photo by Michael Gilroy.

female's cage, but this is more likely to cause fights.

Colonies

I have found that colonies are rarely totally successful, especially for more than a year, without major outside interference and the removal of individuals. It appears that quite a large area is required and at least two females should be present for each male. However, fighting still appears more common in colonies than in pairs.

Each individual should have its own nest box (see Housing). I would also suggest that you provide an extra nest box for every three animals in the colony. A number of hollow logs or pipes on the floor of the cage is also useful to allow submissive animals to escape unwanted attentions from the dominant animals. Quite often, only the most dominant female in a colony will breed and the numbers per litter appear as low as those produced by pairs. The other major problem with colonies is that the exact parentage is difficult to know and it is far more difficult to tame individuals.

A New Husband

On rare occasions, for some reason or another a female will — perhaps due to the death of her original mate — refuse to accept another male. Often at this stage the female has to be left out of the breeding programme or given away as a non-breeding individual. This can be a great disappointment, particularly if she is an unusual colour. However, this does not always have to be the case; there are ways to overcome the problem. For example, a female that has lost her mate but still has her litter or is pregnant will often accept one of her sons as her consort the following spring. This may be achieved by not removing the chosen male with the rest of the litter at weaning. However, care should be taken to monitor her continued acceptance of him. Some females will not accept any male on a permanent basis. Should you find this to be the case, it may be possible to hand mate her. This means allowing her access to a male only when she is on heat and removing him after mating. This is difficult and should only be considered as a last resort. Again the female should be introduced to the male's cage. This should be on the second day of her cycle, the day when she is calling and basically demanding a male to mate with. There may be a slight play fight on meeting but by this time you should be able to tell a serious fight from a mock battle.

New nest boxes are always thoroughly investigated before they are acceptable to the chipmunk.

A male trying desperately to get to the receptive female chipmunk. Photo by Michael Gilroy.

Don't forget: never attempt to stop a fight with bare hands. Should a serious fight occur, remove the female and try her again later the same or next day. As soon as the male has mounted her and copulation has begun, you may leave them alone for a while. Never allow the female, if she is known to attack males, to remain in his cage for longer than a few hours, and never overnight.

Another way of achieving this is to place the female in a small cage within the male's abode where he has access to her odour through the bars of the cage. When the female appears ready to allow the male to mount her, he will usually be tolerated and she can be released. This is also a useful way to introduce a new female to any over-aggressive male.

Single individuals and single-sexed pairs and groups appear to work quite well and are happy when breeding is not required. However, adult individuals of the same sex which previously have been used for breeding are unlikely to tolerate each other.

Finally, don't forget that a male removed from the female and her young may be difficult to reintroduce. Allow the male to stay with the female and her babies; he will rarely harm the young and in fact some males, unlike those in the wild, actually help with their rearing.

Hand Rearing

As far as I am aware, few people have raised baby chipmunks from birth, but it can be done. There is no special preparation available for the hand-rearing of rodents so sadly, to some extent, all hand-rearing is trial and error. All that I can say is that, from the small number of people who have successfully handreared chipmunks, the following appears to work. I am not saying that this is the only way to hand-rear, merely that this method has worked for some.

The most important factor to remember in successful hand-rearing is the need to feed the individual(s) regularly. Animals as small as chipmunks take such tiny amounts of food at any single feed that it is extremely important to maintain the intake of nourishment. However, it is also very important to avoid feeding foods that are too rich. The first sign of an over-rich diet is diarrhoea. Unfortunately, unless the problem is corrected quickly the outcome will be the death of the baby.

Hand-rearing is a time-consuming and very tiring business, and this must be remembered before any attempt is made. Until the baby chipmunk is three weeks old it will require feeding every three hours day and night. At four weeks you may drop the early or middle of the night feeds (between midnight and 6am). If the baby is the runt of the litter, you may need to increase the number of feeds from every three hours to every two until it is four weeks old.

A young chipmunk 36 days old. Photo by Michael Gilroy.

A typical wooden bird's nest box converted to use as a chipmunk's home.

To feed, use a dropper; you can buy one marketed as suitable for very small kittens, and you need the smallest that there is. You must feed the baby very slowly and watch carefully all the time for bubbles coming from its nostrils or the sounds of choking, which indicate that the food is not entering the stomach but the lungs. Should this happen hold the baby gently by the hind legs head down until the lungs are clear again. Between feeds, the animal(s) should be kept in a box, in a nest made of soft tissue paper or cloth and lightly covered to allow the air to get to them. The box must be kept in a warm, but not a hot, place.

After each feed, lightly stroke the baby's stomach. Stroke towards the tail with a warm piece of cotton wool to stimulate the bowels.

SUITABLE DIET

Days 1—7: 1 part of evaporated milk to 2 parts water, with a pinch of glucose powder.

Days 8—30: 4 teaspoons of baby cereal; 1 teaspoon evaporated milk; 0.5 teaspoon of honey or glucose powder. This should be mixed together to the consistency of gruel.

Alternatively you can use a prepared milk-rearing food sold for kittens. When hand-rearing it is useful to know what stage of development should be reached at what time. The following may be of help:

Days 10—12: stripes show on the skin.

Days 12—14: fur begins to appear through the skin.

Day 16: looks like a miniature adult, but still has its eyes closed.

Days 26—30: eyes and ears open.

Days 30—35: solid food taken.

HEALTH

Most chipmunks and other species in this book are healthy throughout their lives, living for quite a long time and eventually dying of old age. Increased inbreeding is likely to cause slight problems, but many problems are caused by bad management: feeding, siting of cages and other forms of stress. I am not saying that chipmunks are never ill, but it is rare.

I shall mention the most common causes of problems and what to do if they occur. However, if your chipmunk appears ill and you are unsure what to do, please do not have a wild guess and try to treat it yourself; take the animal straight to your local veterinary surgeon.

WOUNDS AND CUTS

As with rodents, a chipmunk's flesh heals very quickly, and slight cuts and wounds are not in themselves dangerous at all. The most common cause of these wounds are sharp edges to the climbing, bedding materials, edges to the cage and slight fights. Serious wounds do occur when strange individuals are introduced to each other and at these times great care should be taken. Only very deep wounds or cuts need to be dealt with by a vet. Most cuts can be bathed in a mild antiseptic solution once a day. This may mean removing an individual from an outdoor enclosure or group, unless your animals are very tame and come

A small indoor cage suitable to use as a quarantine cage.

A wire bottom to the chipmunk cage allows the waste to fall through to a litter tray.

to you easily. If your animal is not used to being handled, then it may be worth not treating a very mild wound at all; just keep a very close eye on it for infection and allow nature to heal the wound itself.

CONSTIPATION

A blockage of the intestines causes constipation. In the majority of cases, this is caused by unsuitable bedding such as cotton wool, wood waste and kapok. All bedding should be replaced with good soft meadow hay and fresh foods should be given in larger amounts than usual. Should constipation persist for more than 24 hours, consult your vet.

DIARRHOEA

The opposite of constipation. The most common cause of this is the over-feeding of fresh vegetables and a change in diet. Nursing females tend to produce looser faeces than normal and this is nothing to worry about.

OVERGROWN TEETH

On very rare occasions, the teeth of chipmunks and other rodents become overgrown. This is often caused by the feeding of too much soft food in the diet. The individual should be taken to the vet for the teeth to be trimmed and the animal's diet changed to include a much higher proportion of nuts and biscuits on which the teeth are worn down. Even rarer is the case of misaligned teeth. This can occur in both adults and young when the teeth and jaws have been damaged by an accident or in a fight. In many cases clipping of the teeth will have to be performed once a month and this can cause a great deal of stress to some animals. Should this be the case then it may be kinder to ask your vet to put the animals to sleep.

HIBERNATION

This is not an ailment or illness, but it seems appropriate to mention it here. Chipmunks that are kept outdoors all year without access to heated accommodation often hibernate. This is usually in their nest box or, if they have a peat or soil-based cage, they may well dig burrows. Hibernation does not appear to be harmful to chipmunks and, indeed, in many areas of the wild they hibernate quite naturally. You should bear two things in mind. One: they should be allowed to make a position. Two: that the animals must be given a very good diet during the previous few months in order that they build up a good fat supply on which to live while in hibernation.

For this reason I would not allow newly acquired animals to hibernate - just in case. Chipmunks do not hibernate all winter, but rather for odd days at a time, particularly when the weather is cold and damp.

Patience is required to build up trust between you and your pet chipmunk. When your pet moves his head in the direction of your extended hand or treat (an acorn in this case), you can consider this as progress.

CHOOSING A CHIPMUNK

What age, sex or combination of chipmunks to buy really depend on what you require from them ultimately. I have found that single-sexed groups rarely do well together, although other people have had more success. If breeding is required, obviously you require a pair, one of each sex. These, unless you are buying animals of a rare type or mutation, should be as unrelated as possible.

Breeding animals can be any age up to about two years. If they are not tame at this age, they are not likely to become so, but as breeding animals this is not so important. Be wary of young animals labelled as breeding stock, if they are under two years of age and have not bred. They may be potential breeders, but no one can tell if a pair of animals will settle down to breed. They should be sold as a potential breeding pair.

If you want only a single individual for a pet, then you need an animal that is as young as possible, for example 8—16 weeks. Although some animals over this age tame down very well, it takes longer.

When buying a chipmunk of any type, sex or age, always ensure that you choose one that is lively, with a good shine to its coat. It should have bright eyes and be without cuts and scars. Also make sure that it has a full tail. A damaged tail does a lot to destroy the charm of the species and it may also be the sign of an older or imported animal. This may be acceptable if you require totally unrelated blood for your stud. However, it could also the sign of a fighter. Having said all this, one of my own bought-in animals has no earflaps. They were chewed off when he was very young by his mother. He was a single baby and she just loved to wash and wash him. He is called Vincent after Vincent Van Gogh and has proved to be the best stud male I have. He uses his lack of ears to pretend he can't hear me call with a titbit and then, when his mate has eaten everything, he comes over complaining that he has missed out. In this way he tends to get more treats than anyone else.

CHIPMUNK SPECIES

The following is a list of the various chipmunk species and their distribution in the wild.

Eutamias sibiricus
Siberia, Mongolia, Northern and Central China, Korea and Hokkaido (Japan).

Eutamias aplinus
Sierra Nevadas (east and central California).

Eutamias minimius
Yukon to Ontario and Wisconsin.

Eutamias amoenus
Southwestern Canada and Northwestern USA.

Eutamias townsendii
Extreme southwestern British

Columbia to western Oregon.

Eutamias ochrogenys
  Northwestern coast of California.

Eutamias senex
  Central Oregon and Northern California.

Eutamias siskiyou
  Southwestern Oregon, extreme North Western California

Eutamias sonanae
  Northwestern California.

Eutamias merrimai
  Central and Southern California; Baja California

Eutamias obscurus
  Southern California; Baja California

Eutamias dorsalis
  Southwestern USA, Northern Mexico

Eutamias quadrifittaus
  Eastern Utah, Colorado, Northeast Arizona, New Mexico, extreme Western Oklahoma.

Eutamias ruficaudus
  Southern British Colombia, extreme Southwestern Alberta, Northeastern Washington, and Northern and Northwest Montana.

Eutamias canpies
  South central Mexico, extreme western Texas, probably northern Mexico.

Eutamias cinereicollis
  East central Arizona, South west Mexico

Eutamias quadrimaculatus
  East central California

Eutamias speciosus
  Mountains of Eastern and Southern California.

Eutamias panamintinius
  South West Nevada and adjacent parts of California

Eutamias umbrinus
  West central USA

Eutamias palmeri
  Southern Nevada

Eutamias bulleri
  West Central Mexico

THE WESTERN AMERICAN CHIPMUNK

The head and body length of the various Eutamias species vary from 8—16cm (approximately 3—6in) with the additional tail length of from 6—14cm (2.3—5.5.in). Coat colours vary just as much and I shall deal with each species separately; however, all have conspicuous black or brownish-black longitudinal back stripes separated by whitish or buff stripes. The species vary greatly in both habits and habitats but, in general, the western chipmunks are more arboreal, less shy and more social. Many inhabit overlapping ranges from lowland to mountaintop, with the palest chipmunks originating in the driest areas and the darkest in the most humid.

The following is a list of the species of Eutamias that have been kept in captivity at some time. All can be treated in the same way as the Siberian.

The Alpine Chipmunk
(Eutamias alpinus)

A small species, generally yellowish-grey with dark reddish or brownish side stripes, not black. A dark stripe down the middle of the back is usually black. The tail is bright orange below, approximately 16—20cm (approximately 6—8in) long.

The Least Chipmunk
(Eutamias minimus)

This chipmunk is 16—22.5cm (6—9in) long in total. In the wild state it has a very wide range and consequently variable colouring. In drier areas, it is a muted yellowish-grey above with tan dark stripes; in the moister areas, it is brownish-grey with black side stripes; stripes continue to the base of the tail. Sides are orangish-brown, belly greyish-white. The tail is long, light brown above, yellowish below with hairs tipped black. Ears are noticeably tawny in front. It is the lightest in colour of all the Western Chipmunks.

The Yellow Pine Chipmunk
(Eutamias amoenus)

This is one of the larger species at 18—24.5cm (7—9.6in) and is brightly coloured, ranging from tawny to pinkish-cinnamon, with very distinct stripes. Light stripes are whitish while the dark stripes are usually black. Sides and undersides of the tail are brownish-yellow. The top of the head is brown and the ears are blackish in front and whitish behind.

Townsend's Chipmunk
(Eutamias townsendii)

Another of the larger species at 22—32cm (8.6—12.5in), the Townsend's is dark brown in colour, often with rather wide, diffuse or at least indistinct blackish and light stripes on its head, which continue down the body. It is lighter in summer than in winter. The backs of the ears are noticeably bi-coloured; dusky on the front half, grey on the back. The tail is long and bushy; blackish above with many white-tipped hairs, bridge reddish-brown below bordered with black and finely edged with white-tipped hairs.

The Sonoma Chipmunk
(Eutamias sonomae)

A large and noticeably brownish chipmunk, from 22—28cm (8.6—11in) in length. All the stripes on the back are indistinct, and are all about the same width; lighter stripes are yellowish. The tail is reddish below, but becomes much paler towards the base, edged with buff. On the head, the dark stripes are reddish, with black spots behind the eyes and below the ears. The backs of the ears are nearly uniform brownish in colour.

Merriam's Chipmunk
(Eutamias merriami)

The Merriam's chipmunk is a greyish-brown species, 21—28cm (8.2—11in) long. It has a distinct white belly. The stripes are nearly equal in width but indistinct, the dark stripes are either grey or brown; only rarely black. Lighter stripes greyish. The tail is long, edged with buff or white.

The Cliff Chipmunk

A medium chipmunk, 19.5—28cm (7.6—11in). Greyish in colour, the stripes on the body are either indistinct or totally absent, yet often are quite distinct on the sides of the head. The bushy tail is a rust red below.

The Long Eared Chipmunk
(Eutamias quadrimaculatus)

A fairly large, impressive, brightly-coloured chipmunk with indistinct body stripes. The tail is reddish-brown below edged with white. The ears are long with a large white patch behind and a dark, almost black, stripe below.

HABITS OF THE WESTERN AMERICAN SPECIES

As stated earlier, in order to understand your chipmunk's requirements in captivity, it is necessary to look at its behaviour in the wild. The Western species vary considerably in both habits and habitats but they are more agile and active than both the Eastern American and the Siberian, although on the whole, they are very similar to the Siberian.

As with the Siberian, the Western species dig their burrows in the ground or in old rotting logs. Although they have been closely studied above the ground in some parts of their wide range, little is actually known about any of the species' burrow construction. It appears that the tunnel is about 60—90cm (23.5—35.5in) in length, terminating in a chamber about 30cm (12in) below the ground surface. This small chamber contains a nest as well as a food store of seeds for winter use. Occasionally, some species inhabit holes in trees fairly high up, but this is thought to be quite rare and usually is due to conditions on the ground, such as frequent floods.

It appears that total hibernation occurs only in areas where deep snow lies on the ground all winter, thus preventing the chipmunks' foraging for food. There is generally only a single litter each year; second litters seem to be much rarer than in the Siberian. Vocal calls appear to be the same in all the species and are very similar to the Siberian. As with the Siberian, the Westerns are quite social in both the wild and captivity and thus caging as described for the Siberian is suitable for them.

THE EASTERN AMERICAN CHIPMUNK *(TAMIAS STRIATUS)*

This single species in the wild inhabits the Eastern United States of America and the southeastern areas of Canada. It is a larger species than the others so far mentioned with a body length of 14—19cm (5.5—7.5in) and tail of 8—11cm (3—4in). The background colour varies from reddish-brown to chestnut and there are five black stripes separated by pale stripes; the stripes fade into the reddish flanks and rump. The underparts are white to buff-coloured and the feet are tan. The prominent short ears are edged with russet. The tail is reddish-brown, well furred and yet not bushy. Overall the fur is straight, soft and quite fine.

On the whole the Eastern Chipmunk is rather a solitary species and can be highly aggressive towards others of its own kind, even in the wild. For this reason it is rarely seen in

The stripes on a White chipmunk are pale beige.

captivity. In the wild, each adult defends a small home range. This is usually based around and centred on the burrow, from which all intruders are chased away.

During the breeding season males congregate on the home range of a single female and compete for mating privileges. There are certainly no lasting pair bonds. For this reason Eastern Chipmunks should only be retained together during the short period in which the female is receptive to the male. I recommend that a male is introduced to the female's cage only when she is calling loudly and showing very obvious signs that she is willing to mate. They should be watched very carefully and parted as soon as fighting occurs. If you do not do this, you may well end up with one very dead male. This is not to say that the species cannot be retained in captivity, merely that individuals are more difficult and require a much larger area than the Eutamias species.

As a species the Eastern Chipmunk is much more of a ground dweller, and thus doesn't require quite such a high cage. It is also important that the nest boxes are sited lower down. Diet and development of the young are similar to the Siberian, although after weaning it may be necessary to house each individual in a separate cage.

OTHER SPECIES

This part of the book covers other types of rodents that can be kept in a similar way to the chipmunk. The species that I have chosen may not be everyone's choice, nor may they be as suitable as the chipmunk for some people, but they are very similar in their requirements, with one or two exceptions.

DEGU (OCTODON DEGU)

Three species of degu are recognised in the wild originating from various parts of the Andes mountains but, as far as I am aware, only the above-mentioned species has been and is retained in captivity. The degu is rather difficult to describe, but once you have seen one you will not forget it. It is rather like a small, lightly-built chinchilla, but has a long, almost hairless, tail and a pointed face. Its overall size is approximately 12.5—19.5cm (5—7.6in), so it is not large. The upper parts are greyish or brownish with an orange tinge, with lighter markings at the neck and the underparts tending to fade towards a more creamy colour. The ears are relatively large and the tail quite long, terminating in a black tuft. Care must be taken when handling the degu, as the tail is very fragile and can be shed if the animal is roughly handled or grabbed by the tail. Once lost, the tail will not regrow. Degu also resent being caught by the tail and are very likely to bite when handled other than by being cupped, or gently but firmly held around the body.

When a degu bites, which is not often, they mean it and bite hard, making sure it hurts by not letting go too soon. Having said this, degu are not animals that bite for the sake of it. If given a lot of time and attention, they become very tame and come to you when they are called.

Degu are very vocal animals and talk a lot among themselves in a series of squeaks and whistles. Once they get to know you, you will be included in their chat. However, if a stranger is around, once the alarm calls have been given they will remain very firmly hidden away. They certainly do not like noisy visitors to the home.

Caging for degu is even easier than for chipmunks. They should be housed indoors, or in an outdoor shed that is heated in the winter. They can be retained in outdoor cages in the summer but, on the whole, they do not do well in them. I suggest that they are kept in a large cage as described for the indoor chipmunks. However, if you do not have the room for such a large cage, a good alternative is a very large aquarium. This should be at least 120 x 45 x 45cm (48 x 18 x 18in) and is suitable for a pair and their young. Of course, it should be fitted with a mesh top.

However you decide to keep them, the cage or aquarium should be furnished with a good amount of things which the degu can climb and hide in. They are great gnawers and will chew a wooden nest box to pieces in a matter of hours should they decide that it is better in smaller bits. Because of this I usually provide them with earthenware pipes in which they can nest and hide and thick branches on which to climb. The floor should be given a deep bed of shaving litter and lots of soft meadow hay in which they can nest, hide and eat.

Degu are very social animals and they do not enjoy being kept on their own. They are best retained in pairs or small family groups. Although all female groups will live together, it is thought that, if a non-breeding group is wanted, all male groups are best. They are not generally difficult to get together and adult animals of the opposite sex usually accept each other with little difficulty. It has been suggested that a female will not come into heat without the presence of the male. Gestation is 90 days and the young are born fully furred with their eyes almost fully open. They are weaned at 14—21 days although they try solid food from about day 7. Some females allow the young to wander from the nest from a very early age while others confine

Degus are social animals and they greatly enjoy company.

them for the first week or so. The litters are large and range from 1—10 individuals. You can expect your degu to live for about six or seven years, if it is kept correctly.

The diet of the species is always an area of disagreement and here I shall tell you what I have found successful. My animals are given a daily diet of a good rodent mix, which contains a wide variety of seeds, nuts, cereals, grains and dried vegetables. In addition to this, every other day they are given fresh root vegetables such as carrot, swede, parsnip, and their favourite, sweet potato. On very rare occasions they are given very small amounts of apple or grapes. This is the area that causes the disagreement as many people say that fruit is bad for their system and that it should never be fed. It does appear that the problem is only caused by fresh, and not dried fruit. On the whole, I play safe and feed very small amounts very rarely. In the spring and summer I give small amounts of fresh grass and that which is not eaten is usually used for bedding. Fresh soft meadow hay is always available, as is water.

THE SOUTHERN FLYING SQUIRREL (GLAUCOMYS VOLANS)

The next species that we are going to look at is the opposite to the Degu. The Flying Squirrel is a very nocturnal animal.

Although there are many types of Flying Squirrel in the wild, as far as I am aware the Southern Flying Squirrel is the only species that has been retained in captivity to any extent. It is a beautiful creature, very shy and retiring until it gets to know you but, once used to you, it can be very tame providing that you are willing to wait until it is ready to wake up. The species is found in the wild from southeastern Canada, the eastern United States and south to Mexico and Honduras.

They are small, being only about 22—27cm (8.6—10.6in) long, and the females are larger than the males. Their nocturnal habits are reflected by their large, black eyes. The fur is soft and thick; in colour it is an ashy-grey above and creamy-white below.

The term 'flying' is applied to these animals because they have a fold of skin, extending from the wrist to the ankles, which enables them to make long, gliding leaps from tree to tree. The skin acts more like a parachute to slow down the animal; it can not be flapped like a bat's wings. Many people think that because of this ability, Flying Squirrels ought to be provided with a very large cage so that they can glide form one end to the other. In fact, this is far from the case. Flying Squirrels do not do so well in large cages as they do in smaller ones. Any of the cages that are suitable for the chipmunks are suitable for the Flying Squirrel. They are equally at home indoors or in outdoor aviaries. However, it must be remembered that if they are retained outdoors, you are unlikely to see very much of them as they will only emerge from their nests once it is dark.

Cages should be furnished in much the same way as for chipmunks, with branches to climb on, a base of wood shavings, and soft meadow hay for nesting materials. A nest box should be supplied for each individual; they do not like large, spacious boxes so those designed for budgies are ideal. These should be placed as high up in the cage as possible. I usually allow just enough space between the roof of the nest box and the roof of the cage for an adult animal to sit on to watch what is going on around it.

A wide variety of foods can be offered to this species but you may find that the animals settle for three or four basic food items and anything else is regarded as treats. Having said this, a balanced diet should be offered. I usually feed a basic seed diet as described for the chipmunks but to this I add various items that I know the Flying Squirrels are fond of. These can consist of various forms of nuts, pecan, hazel, peanuts, brazil, almond, walnuts and acorns. They will also eat a small amount of the same fruit and vegetables as the chipmunks. They appreciate small amounts of insect foods at certain times of the year, including mealworms and crickets. I have watched my own animals catch and eat moths and spiders that have wandered into their cage.

Flying Squirrels rarely do anything slowly, except perhaps wake up. Their movements are quick and they rarely walk, rather scampering and jumping about. Understand this and you will be able to handle them. Even newly-acquired adult animals can be tamed and handled as long as you have a lot of patience and do not try to start the taming process until the animal has settled in its new home. As with the chipmunk, a new Flying Squirrel is easier to handle when it is hungry and, by using food as a reward, you will soon be able to encourage the animal to get used to you and your hands. Talk to your animals; yes, this may sound strange, but they react very well to the human voice and will soon learn that the sound of your voice means that food is about to arrive. Encourage the animal to take an item of food

from your hand and, while it is sitting eating, gently stroke its back. To begin with it will usually retreat away from you, so try to place your hand between it and the nest box. In order to eat the food it will have to go to a corner rather than back inside. Gently stoke the neck and the top of the head; for some reason the Flying Squirrel particularly seems to like this. After a few stokes, allow the animal to go for more food and continue again. After a while you will find that it is sniffing your fingers and has realised that you are not going to harm it. Continue this for a few nights and then you can stroke the ears and neck of the animal. While doing this, move your thumb under the chin and in front of the legs and the other fingers around the body, leaving only the tail free, and lift. The grip should be firm but gentle. The squirrel will struggle but rarely bite, so stroke the ears and head as you have been doing and talk to it. After a few moments open your hand and let it back into the cage. Continue the same thing again for a few nights and, eventually, you will find that the Squirrel will jump on to your hand, run up your arm and around your shoulders. At this point you can let it roam around the room. Remember to close all doors and windows and make sure that the family cat and dog are out of the way.

Flying Squirrels can be kept in a variety of groupings, including pairs and small colonies. Some people say that a single Squirrel is quite happy and this is true, but

A typical flying squirrel. Flying squirrels make great pets. This kind of flying squirrel is called a _sugar glider_. Photo by Ralph Lermeyer.

then it does require a lot more attention from its owner, or it will get very lonely.

The most successful way to keep this species is in pairs. They usually breed in the autumn in the year after they were born. Conception usually takes place in the late autumn and the litter is born in February. Towards the end of January the female begins to be rather temperamental and is noticeably short-tempered with her husband, chasing and generally making his life uneasy. Should the male become very harassed by the female then it is probably best to remove him to another cage for a few weeks. Don't worry, she will accept him back again. The female begins to gather her nesting materials and then she usually disappears from sight for a day or so. This is when the babies are born. Do not disturb them.

A litter usually consists of 2—4 young, although there can be more. They are born naked and blind. They are very slow-growing at first, but at two weeks they are covered in fur, at three weeks their eyes are open and at four weeks they are out of the nest and you can begin to handle them. If the female allows the father to stay in the cage then they will both sleep with and protect the young.

The young may be removed from the parents at eight weeks and housed separately, or they can be left with the parents for longer. If the babies are removed a female that has littered in February will produce another litter in July. If a female is later with her litter and has the first in May, then usually she will have a second in September. I do not know of any female that has produced more than two litters in a year.

DORMICE

Dormice of one species or another have been kept in captivity for many centuries, and there is evidence that they were commonly used as food by the Romans. Today they are becoming quite popular as pets. There are a number of different species throughout the world; of these, three are quite common as pets, one is rarely retailed and one is very rare as it is governed by wild-life conservation laws.

The Edible or Fat Dormouse *(Glis glis)*, ranges from France and Northern Spain to the Volga River and northern Iran, as well as some of the islands in the Mediterranean. It was introduced into the English countryside in the early 1900s. It is the largest of the species, with a head and body length of 15—18cm (6—7in) and a bushy tail of 13—16cm (5—6in). In colour it is a silvery-grey above, light grey to white below, with a ring of black hair around the small, black eyes. The silver-grey tail has a parting on the under-side which is lighter in colour.

The African Dormouse *(Graphiurus murinus)* is found throughout Africa, south of the Sahara Desert. The smallest of the species, it averages only 7cm (2.7in). It is very similar in colour to the Edible, although the belly fur is usually much more noticeably white.

The Forest Dormouse *(Drymoys nitedula)* is found through central Europe to Iran. The head and body length is about 8—13cm (3—5in). The general coloration is greyish to yellowish-brown on the upper parts and buff-white on the underparts. The bushy tail is a similar colour to the body.

The Garden Dormouse *(Eliomys quercinus)* ranges from France and Spain to the Urals, including North Africa. The head and body length is 10—17.5cm (4—6.8in), with a tail of 9—13.5cm (3.5—5.3in). The fur on the body is shorter than the other species but much longer at the tip of the tail, where it forms a long tuft. The general colour of the upper parts ranges through several grey and brown shades. The underparts are white and the face generally has some black markings. In the European populations the tail is distinctively tri-coloured on top, having a cinnamon-brown half nearest the body, followed by a black third and ending in a distinct white tip.

The Common or Hazel Dormouse *(Muscardinus avellanrius)* is found from France and southern Sweden to European Russia and northern Asia Minor. It is found in the United Kingdom but is becoming very rare and is subject to the endangered species laws. It is quite small, with a head and body length of only 8—8.5cm (3—3.3in). In coloration, it is a distinct orange, chestnut brown with pale buff underparts and a white throat patch.

With the exception of the African Dormouse, which is a very small species that I shall deal with later, the housing for the dormice is the same as that for the chipmunks. Like Flying Squirrels, all Dormice tend to be nocturnal.

In captivity, as in the wild, they rarely move about on the ground if they can get from A to B without doing so. They therefore require many more branches to climb about on than the other species mentioned in this book. Dormice are very skilled climbers and gnawers and can be very destructive, especially in all-wooden cages. They are not an easy group of animals to handle but they do become very tame and will climb on you and take food from your hands. Edible Dormice will even come when called. Unlike most rodent species, the dormouse male is aggressive to humans more than the female and I have rarely found a male, particularly in the Edibles, that is 100% safe. I never totally trust my Edible males, as they are likely to give a nip just to let you remember who is boss.

All the species in the wild tend to be nocturnal and solitary, except in the winter when they gather on one nest site, presumably to stay warmer. In captivity, however, once they have settled down this can and does change. All can easily be retained in sexed pairs. Each animal should be provided with a nest box and, if the cage is big enough,

I usually place an additional nest box in as well.

Dormice eat a vast amount of different foods: seeds, cereals, nuts and berries as well as insects, and some species enjoy flowers and nectar. Sugar water and honey is very much enjoyed by them, particularly in the spring just after hibernation. Food bowls should not be placed on the floor of the cage. Some species such as the Edible will come down to the floor for food but, once they have dropped something, they do not think to look for it below. For this reason, they tend to waste much of the food given to them. Diet is important as they need to put on a lot of fat reserves in the summer and autumn if they are to be allowed to hibernate.

There are various opinions as to whether or not they should be allowed to hibernate in captivity and, if so, whether or not this affects their breeding the following year. At present this is unclear. What is clear, however, is that a fat individual in spring will rarely breed but, on the other hand, nearly 25% of individuals allowed to hibernate will not survive the winter. This figure is not so high as some species.

Dormice can be lazy animals. Even though the Hazel Dormouse is famous for its love of hazel nuts, in captivity it may refuse to gnaw into the shell to extract the nut when other food is available. Water should be available at all times.

Dormice usually have a single litter a year in the late spring, although more people are finding that captive animals produce a second litter in the early autumn. In the wild this litter would rarely survive the winter. Generally the habits are similar for all the different species. Once wide awake from hibernation, the male courts the female by following her around the cage or aviary uttering a very soft twittering sound until she allows him to mate. Once pregnant, the female may attack the male and you may have to remove him until the litter is weaned. This is more common in the smaller species than the Edible where pairs usually stay together much more often.

The dormouse, known scientifically as *Glis glis*, will gorge on apples in the autumn

The female usually takes a great deal of bedding into the nest box and does not allow the male in. The young are born blind and naked after a gestation of 30 days; depending on the species the litter can contain from 1—9 individuals. They are weaned at 30 days but are often out of the nest exploring the world a few days before this. Some females move their babies from one nest to another during the growth period so it is important to provide an extra nest box at this time. The Garden Dormouse keeps her young with her for slightly longer than the other species and they can often be seen moving around the cage head to tail rather like a file of elephants.

THE AFRICAN DORMOUSE

This species is much smaller than the other species and also more delicate. For this reason the dormice should be housed differently. I suggest that you use a large aquaria, a good size would be 1120 x 60 x 60cm (4 x 2 x 2ft). This should be equipped with a good-fitting wire mesh top, a deep litter base and small nest boxes. In my experience, the African Dormouse can be retained in small colonies, and then I provide a nest box for every two animals. However, some people say that the males are too aggressive with each other and that colonies do not work. Like their bigger cousins, the African Dormice require a lot of climbing area but, unlike the larger ones, they also enjoy digging in the shavings and therefore I provide quite a deep litter for this activity. Diet is as for the bigger species with the addition of more small seeds such as canary seed.